SUNDAY EXPRESS & DAILY EXPRESS
CARTOONS

Forty-first Series

AN EXPRESS BOOKS PUBLICATION

© 1987 Express Newspapers p.l.c., Fleet Street, London, EC4P 4JT
Printed in Great Britain by Richard Clay Ltd, Bungay, Suffolk

U·K £2·25

Photograph by Richard Young.

FOREWORD

by

JOAN

COLLINS

Giles. Whenever I hear that name, it conjures up visions of England. An England that hasn't changed very much since I was a child giggling at the antics of Grandma, mum and dad, the kids, and all the other favourite beloved characters that he created so brilliantly.

A Giles cartoon isn't like any other cartoon. It is deeply detailed with subtly hidden humours lurking in every corner. It is indeed a veritable gem to study and laugh at with the morning tea.

I often feel that the only character who could ever get the better of Alexis* would be Grandma.

Now *there's* an idea for a cartoon! Are you listening Carl?

With Love
Joan C.

*N.B: For those of you who don't know, Alexis is a vicious, scheming, naughty person that I play in Dynasty. Oh Grandma, we'd *love* to have you in it!

"The one you knocked down to a pint a day, Doctor—she's keeping count of every gin I serve you."

Daily Express, June 26th, 1986

"George, your wife's calling you—you're playing the winners."

Sunday Express, June 29th, 1986.

"He holds that none of them have beaten the Cutty Sark yet, under sail."

Daily Express, July 1st, 1986

"If you're going to keep on about missing the punch-ups between McEnroe and the umpires,
we're glad you're not coming."

Daily Express, July 3rd, 1986

"She's sent me home to put some teeth in and a tie on in case Prince Charles calls on the hop."

Sunday Express, July 6th, 1986

"Owing VAT on bonuses for winning has never been a problem for you, has it?"

Daily Express, July 8th, 1986

"They had the same problems when they allowed women cricketers into Lords."

Daily Express, July 10th, 1986

"I'll do my best not to win, but if I lose I'll knock the stuffing out of you."

(Headline: Head bans competition in school)

Sunday Express, July 13th, 1986

"If many more of them back out, bang goes my new Rover."

Daily Express, July 15th, 1986

"Monday: Cricket—Scouts v. Sea Cadets, our house, lunch one o'clock. Tuesday: Baseball—our house, early buffet lunch, tea, four o'clock. Wednesday . . ."

Daily Express, July 17th, 1986

"'Be prepared', as they taught me in the Scouts."

"Another reason we hope you won't be sitting here tomorrow—your embrocation is upsetting our tracker dogs."

Daily Express, July 22nd, 1986

"This new Geldof gear—I'm having trouble with the 'at."

Sunday Express, July 27th, 1986

"Guinness were going to pay me £2m for advertising on the back of my pants until yon Viscount Gough told the world we don't wear any."

Daily Express, July 29th, 1986

"No it does NOT make me happier to know the people next door have gone on a camping holiday as well!"

Daily Express, August 5th, 1986

"I know our little man is not a member of the Squadron, but just in case HRH comes in your fish bar."

(*Headline: Their Royal Highnesses visited tourist country in Spain*)

Daily Express, August 7th, 1986

"We don't often get punch-ups on this ferry—unless somebody refuses to vacate this lady's favourite seat right now."

Sunday Express, August 10th, 1986

"Hullo, hero boy—I'd take Dad's United shirt off if I was you. He's got some sort of 'Welcome Home' party arranged."

Daily Express, August 12th, 1986

"Polo, be a good dog and tell us where you've hidden the lady you took for walkies."

(*Headline: Polo the Spaniel takes P.M. for walk*)

Daily Express, August 14th, 1986

"This explains why he brought me early morning tea—he's not going to pay the thieving moguls another 7p a gallon."

Sunday Express, August 17th, 1986

"I wish Dad wouldn't be so pro-Botham in front of the children."

Daily Express, August 19th, 1986

"Why do I think my husband is drunk in charge of a lawnmower? Because he's cutting the wrong lawn for a start!"

Daily Express, August 21st, 1986

"Stop calling him that every time we come past—it's not his fault your team lost their first game!"

Sunday Express, August 24th, 1986

"Ready, dear?"

Daily Express, August 28th, 1986

"Laugh away, Georgie boy—your turn next."

"Tell Miss Babysitter she is about to become redundant."

(*Headline: Gorillas make good baby sitters*)

Daily Express, September 4th, 1986

"I'm not leaving here until it gets dark."

Sunday Express, September 7th, 1986

"Frank's little joke—'For not wearing a seat belt it is the duty of this court to send you to a place where you will be hanged by the neck until you are dead'"

Sunday Express, September 14th, 1986

"I wore my monocle and told the C.O. that our breakfast was cold again and he said: 'Shove orf'"

(With apologies to the Monacled Mutineer)

Daily Express, September 16th, 1986

"Never mind where I come in the Anne Diamond ratings of mixed-up Macho males—get my tea, woman."

Daily Express, September 18th, 1986

"I'm not suggesting nothin'—I'm simply saying my watch was hanging there when Princess Anne looked in and when she'd gone it wasn't."

Sunday Express, September 21st, 1986

"How do they tie 'Bring us our bows, arrers, spears, chariots of fire' with the peace talks in Stockholm?"

Daily Express, September 23rd, 1986

"Poor little Willie spent all his money on a nice new chain ... now they won't let him in to play with it."

Daily Express, September 25th, 1986

"It would be extremely bad for Mrs Currie's health if she came in here—their wives have put 'em all on her Southern diet—lettuce and carrot juice."

Sunday Express, September 28th, 1986

"Here comes her Ladyship—'Exterminate! Exterminate! All red roses OUT!'"

(*Headline: Labour Party adopt the Red Rose for their emblem*)

Daily Express, September 30th, 1986

"Don't be so pessimistic, Grandma—not everything on TV ends with one of them standing the other one up at the altar."

(Headline: 'Eastenders' Michelle jilts Lofty)

Daily Express, October 2nd, 1986

"Underneath their rugged exteriors lies a little pair of silk panties as recommended by Princess Diana."

Sunday Express, October 5th, 1986

"The PM says you can slip it off while she drinks her carrot juice, but back it goes before she puts a foot in the conference hall."

Daily Express, October 7th, 1986

"Richard, before you leave for school, Mother wants me to have a few words about the birds and the bees."

Daily Express, October 9th, 1986

"I suppose that puts Ho Flong in pole position on the rank at the airport."

Sunday Express, October 12th, 1986

"Yes, I read that the Queen had 12 courses for one meal. Here, it's still one course—spare ribs and fried rice, £2.50."

Daily Express, October 14th, 1986

"Take it easy John—the Royal College of Psychiatrists says that more than three halves of beer can seriously damage your health."

Daily Express, October 16th, 1986

"That'll make the Post Office sit up—she's just posted a rude letter to Prince Philip in Hong Kong without a stamp."

Sunday Express, October 19th, 1986

"Don't say it, Philip—please don't say *anything*!"

Daily Express, October 21st, 1986

"It would take more than a big bang in the City to wake our Florrie."

Daily Express, October 28th, 1986

"You realise you are desecrating the image of one of the great freedom fighters who sought to free us from the Capitalist yoke."

Sunday Express, November 2nd, 1986

"It will be extremely bad for our pet's health if I catch him in my bed."

Daily Express, November 4th, 1986

"Some expressions of freedom still have their place in the home, Miss Engels—you're making our chairman blush."

Daily Express, November 6th, 1986

"She claims she rescued Winston Churchill when she was a WAAF in the Boer War."

Sunday Express, November 9th, 1986

"We're sorry about the extra hour's wait—Doctor's had an epidemic of election fever."

Daily Express, November 11th, 1986

"Never mind about serve me right for hiding up a tree all night to catch him coming home from his pub—call the Fire Brigade!"

(*Headline: Shop thy neighbour*)

Sunday Express, November 16th, 1986

"One of them could be Jean Rook, which could be troublesome."

Daily Express, November 18th, 1986

"I know you're a bit niggly this week, Margaret, but I only laid them on your desk for a few seconds."

Daily Express, November 20th, 1986

"With Christmas shoppers in mind don't you think you might try something in the Constable style."

Sunday Express, November 23rd, 1986

"I'm trying to work out her arithmetic—she buys a half dozen British Gas shares then leaves her gasfire on all day so they make a profit."

Daily Express, November 25th, 1986

"Was Michael being economical with the truth when he said he was late for Sunday School because he had to help with the washing up?"

Sunday Express, November 30th, 1986

"Are you the party who let the animals loose from the Smithfield? I'd go and move your bikes if I were you."

Daily Express, December 2nd, 1986

"Madam, there's not enough sex in the world to get you off 132 mph in a 40 limit area."

(*Headline: "Young women should be nice to our policemen" says Judge*)

Daily Express, December 4th, 1986

"Yes, I read Cloughie says footballers are worth £2,400 a week, but there's a wee gap between Station Road Rangers and Bryan Robson."

Sunday Express, December 7th, 1986

"This year's play has nothing that a couple of scenes from The Singing Detective couldn't improve."

Daily Express, December 9th, 1986

"Hide the amplifiers and speakers at your house, Sue—I haven't told Dad I've invited the Hell Bashers Group here for Christmas."

Sunday Express, December 14th, 1986

"And that's my husband—giving us a hand carrying our food mountain."

Daily Express, December 16th, 1986

"In the right corner—Nimrod, AWACS, early warning systems. In the left corner—MI5, EEC, and AIDS etc."

Daily Express, December 18th, 1986

"It's my missus—she wants to know after 54 years in the stables what happened to my £5m Swiss bank account."

(*Headline: Jockeys fortune found in Swiss bank*)

Sunday Express, December 21st, 1986

"Hold tight, Dad—someone's just found a pre-Christmas sale ticket on that bed jacket you gave her."

Sunday Express, December 28th, 1986

"Thank you so much for calling and advising me on the changes I must make in 1987. Now hop it."

Daily Express, December 30th, 1986

"I bet the Japs and Germans don't have to suffer two weeks' Christmas holiday whether they want it or not."

Daily Express, January 1st, 1987

"For the bad news—you've just winged Prince Philip. For the good news—the TV news people are on strike."

Sunday Express, January 4th, 1987

"You've been back one whole day since Christmas—so you'd like two days off to recuperate at the Boat Show."

Daily Express, January 6th, 1987

"My old man runs on about Prince Edward going soft, but we know who has to go out in the cold to get the milk in this house."

Daily Express, January 8th, 1987

"I think Rex is trying to tell us you didn't put the handbrake on."

Sunday Express, January 11th, 1987

"Same thing every year—always makes me late for the Boat Show."

Daily Express, January 13th, 1987

"Grandma's making sure she gets her extra £5 worth."

(*Headline: O.A.P's given increase for fuel*)

Sunday Express, January 18th, 1987

"Great! Here cometh the plumber who charged me £75 to come and look at my burst pipe."

Daily Express, January 20th, 1987

"Thin as a rake—thick as a plank—Prince Charles is still lucky he saw her first!"

Daily Express, January 22nd, 1987

"You bet I'm shouting! Everyone's making as many calls as they can before the BT strike begins!"

Sunday Express, January 25th, 1987

"In case you're interested—it's also the Chinese Year of the Rabbit."

Daily Express, January 27th, 1987

"You won't get off light with this one—he sentenced one of 'em yesterday to six months travel on B.R."

Daily Express, February 5th, 1987

"Come in Corporal—we have a Mrs McGinty who insists that even if we're leaving Ireland YOU'RE staying here!"

Daily Express, February 10th, 1987

"Who's going to tell him his country cottage is about to be replaced by a bingo
hall and a block of high-rise flats?"

Daily Express, February 12th, 1987

"Tell Fifi it was not my idea to bring the wife—it was Madame Edwina Currie."

(*Headline: Government advice "Take wife on business trips"*)

Sunday Express, February 15th, 1987

"I'm jotting down a list of all the ones who aren't laughing their heads off."

Daily Express, February 17th, 1987

"Bertie never thought about this sort of thing until he saw Mary Whitehouse's anti-porn film."

Daily Express, February 19th, 1987

"If the Honourable member of the public directed her political expressions to one party only it would help the peace."

Sunday Express, February 22nd, 1987

"What a thing to ask in front of the children—'Would I rather be the first woman priest or win the Best Bum of the Year contest!'"

Daily Express, February 24th, 1987

"Mrs Jones just told me you're slipping little love notes in the kitty for the new vicar."

Sunday Express, March 1st, 1987

"Her age-group still get prescriptions free so she can afford to sell cut-price."

Daily Express, March 5th, 1987

"It's the dawn chorus of smokers' coughs I shall miss most."

Sunday Express, March 8th, 1987

"In view of the outbreak of politicians' tearoom punch-ups, this is 'Dinger,' our new bouncer, M'Lady."

Sunday Express, March 15th, 1987

"Hard to think of our very own Mr Plod as a sex-frolic Rambo, boozing all night and doing the till."

(*Headline: Night duty police in sex and drink scandal*)

Daily Express, March 17th, 1987

"Yesterday they were hesitating, then along comes Lawson's 2p off income tax . . . . . !"

Daily Express, March 19th, 1987

"In the Spring a young man's fancy lightly turns to thoughts of love! You had any thoughts on the matter Romeo?"

Sunday Express, March 22nd, 1987

"Morning, Bungalow Bill—Joan Collins has just made your tea."

Daily Express, March 24th, 1987

"She says she hasn't missed the opening of the Flat since she was eight."

Daily Express, March 26th, 1987

"50p's worth of flowers and not too many orchids or red roses—his father used to make that joke with me 40 years ago."

Sunday Express, March 29th, 1987

"The faster they step up the Peace Talks, the faster he digs."

Daily Express, March 31st, 1987

"Letter from a lady who says if you're not in the first three on Saturday, hanging'll be too good for you."

(*Headline: Commons say NO to hanging*)

Daily Express, April 2nd, 1987

"Not quite in the Duchess of Windsor bracket—I'll give you £1.50 for the lot."

"Not *another* Japanese gadget? He already calls me 'The Mikado'."

Daily Express, April 7th, 1987

"I'd quit this underpaid job if I wasn't dedicated to scrubbing your sweet little neck every morning."

Daily Express, April 9th, 1987

"His excuse this year—it's against his principles to start on the lawn with our old unpatriotic Jap mower."

Sunday Express, April 12th, 1987

"Her council won't give her boy a car to go fishing during the holidays—how the hell
did this get as far as the Appeal Court?"

(*Headline: Court orders boy to walk to school*)

Daily Express, April 16th, 1987

"Trafford—kindly tell that Guide my private TV quarters are strictly out of bounds to tourists."

Sunday Express, April 19th, 1987

"I wish you'd learn that when somebody asks you: 'Did you have a nice Easter?' you can't just knock them down."

Daily Express, April 21st, 1987

"Who shouted 'Try kicking his backside'?"

Daily Express, April 23rd, 1987

"It's a beautiful poem of undying love, the flowers are wonderful, but I'm still
not letting you have a fiver till Friday."

Sunday Express, April 26th, 1987

"They'll get hey nonny nonny if one of 'em lands on Grandma's foot."

Sunday Express, May 3rd, 1987

"Ah, there you are, Bertie—just in time to save the innings."

Sunday Express, May 10th, 1987

"And I tell you I distinctly remember putting my bike in here last year!"

Sunday Express, May 17th, 1987

"You'd bawl all night if you'd been kissed all day by politicians."

Daily Express, May 21st, 1987

"And my Party's manifesto will remove the BBC's ban on playing George Michael's sex record till after 9 o'clock."

Sunday Express, May 24th, 1987

"To think we came all this way to get away from Party Election Broadcasts."

Daily Express, May 26th, 1987

"The Taverners say Pakistani batsmen having a go at Pakistani hooligans is one thing—Colonel Cholmondley of the Bengal Lancers having a go is another."

Daily Express, May 28th, 1987

"Just bought a lorry load of offensive weapons as used by all the best cricket fans."

"No, it's not West German, it's not Russian—it's Reggie back from fishing in time for the Derby."

(*Headline: Mystery plane lands in Red Square*)

Sunday Express, June 2nd, 1987

"Never mind who I'm voting for—which of them let you in here?"

Sunday Express, June 7th, 1987

"Nice honeymoon in romantic Venice—first night in the nick!"

(Headline: Top security for Mrs. Thatcher in Venice)

Daily Express, June 9th, 1987

"In case you've voted for Screaming Lord Sutch—he's not running."

Daily Express, June 11th, 1987

"That figures—you put a parking ticket on H.R.H.'s car so he taps you on the ankle every time he passes."

Sunday Express, June 14th, 1987

"They've come straight to Ascot from filming 'It's a Knockout'."

Daily Express, June 16th, 1987

"I was thinking more on the lines of hospitals like in Dynasty."

Daily Express, June 18th, 1987

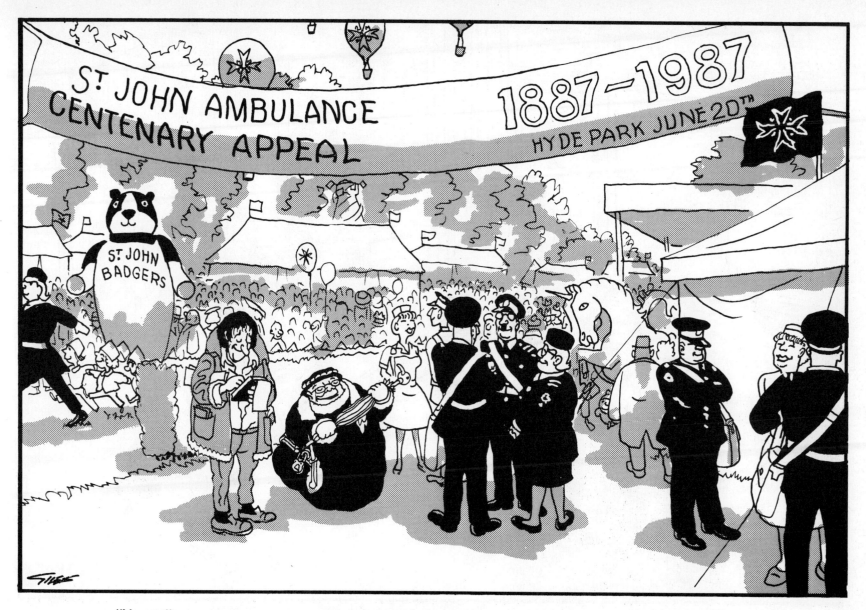

"You tell me once more you expect I was at their opening ceremony and you'll be needing them."

Sunday Express, June 21st, 1987

"Grandma—explain to man's best friend that Man has taken the day off to go to Wimbledon."

Daily Express, June 23rd, 1987

"Thatsh Domocrashy—our gloryish Queen, this very day, is right in there fighting for a Bill to keep you open all day!"

Daily Express, June 25th, 1987

"Boris Becker doesn't behave like that if he loses."

Sunday Express, June 28th, 1987